Pet
Brittany Spaniel

Table of Contents

Pet
Brittany Spaniel

by

Evelyn Monte

Your Brittany's Health

by

George Whitney, D.V.M.

All-Pets Books, Inc.
Fond du Lac, Wisconsin
1959

Drawings
by
Ed Stevenson

Topographical Drawing
(page 77) by
Lloyd Sanford

Character And History

The Brittany spaniel is such an adaptable little dog. Traditionally a hunting dog, he fits just as happily into the role of companion and house pet. And, because he is of smallish size, he is easy to keep in the home, even in a small apartment, and to tuck comfortably on the seat of the car when the family goes on a motor trip.

His smallness, however, is no gauge of his endurance and stamina. He will hunt all day or days on end with the sportsmen of the family and do his part valiantly on pheasant, grouse, woodcock or quail. Many Brittanys are also adept water dogs, if given the experience and training, and will retrieve waterfowl for the gunner or balls for the children.

Perhaps this seems like a large order for a dog weighing a little more than thirty pounds and standing about nineteen inches high when grown, but he would not be a Breton if he were not able to meet the ruggedness of life as well as its comforts with complete equanimity.

The Brittany has two distinctive characteristics that set him apart from other sporting breeds. Although a spaniel, he has an inherent pointing instinct and, unlike the cocker and English springer spaniel which "spring" or flush their game from the cover, the Brittany ranges over the ground and points game as the setters and pointers do. He is the only spaniel breed known in this country which has this strongly developed instinct.

The other distinctive characteristic of the Brittany is his looks. With his ears set high and held well cocked, his generally keen and alert look, he has a very different expression from that of any other spaniel or setter. And this very expression rather denotes his character. He has plenty of fire and go, yet is neither nervous nor high strung. He is cocky, giving no quarter to dogs twice his size for grit and determination, but still retains the calm of an understanding companion.

The Brittany has a natural reserve. When it is pronounced (as it may be in certain individuals) this might sometimes be taken for timidity. But the average Brittany is not at all shy. As a rule he is just not the kind of dog that wants to climb in your lap or show a demanding affection. Rather, he will show his devotion by lying nearby, watching and awaiting your mood. He is sensitive, not very demonstrative and perhaps even a little stand-offish with strangers. His eyes are only for "his family."

One thing is sure, a temperamentally unsound Brittany is such a rarity as to be practically unknown. Probably this is so because they have long been used for the dual purpose of hunting and companion in the home so there is little of the nervous instability that often shows up over a period of time in breeds where inherent instincts are frustrated. If a Brittany is shy or nervous it can be attributed to faults in treatment or training.

Like most dogs of the hunting breeds, he has a quick intelligence, good judgement and the ability to learn. He can be trained for whatever you want to make of him and he will return your affection with all his eager, tough little heart.

Establishing the antiquity of a breed always seems to be a rather vain undertaking in more ways than one. It is, perhaps, the vanity of the owner who takes pride in the fact that his dog comes from one of the oldest known breeds. It is also vain in the meaning that if a breed is ancient at all, it is almost impossible to penetrate the mists of time and find the exact date when it was created.

Some students of the Brittany spaniel claim that it can point to greater antiquity than is commonly believed, and, indeed, offer rather substantial evidence. In a poem by Oppien, who lived about 150 A.D., there is a passage translated by Bellin de Ballu and found in the Strasburg Academic Library in 1787, which reads "among the animals who track-hunt there is an excellent kind, small, that are bred by the savage people of Brittany and are named Agasses. It is mostly by the sensitiveness of its scent that the Agasses takes precedence over other dogs." According to the travels of Oppien it is fairly well established that he referred to the Brittany of France and not the Brittany of England.

Be that as it may, no one knows exactly how or when the first Brittany spaniel was created. It is known, however, that the people of Brittany, that extension of France between the Bay of Biscay and the English Channel, had small local spaniels which excelled so at hunting that visiting sportsmen brought with them dogs of other breeds for mating with the "Epagneul Bretagne." One story is that M. de Mollon, a great French hunter, who came to the region of Coray to live, had Scotch terriers which he mated to the dogs of Brittany, their offspring having a good deal to do with the Brittany's ancestry. It is believed that an Irish setter, "pale in color," which had won a prize at the Paris Exhibition was brought to Brittany for the purpose of mating to the native dogs. There were, at the same time, matings to English dogs, probably English Setters, Welsh Springers, and Pointers.

There is evidence that the early spaniel of the region inherited some of its qualities from the red and white Irish setters which preceded the all-red setters of Ireland. It is noted in history, itself, that when the Irish chieftains invaded Gaul in the fifth century they took their hunting dogs with them.

It has often been stated that the first "tail-less" Brittany spaniel was born about a hundred years ago in a little town in the Valley of Douron, the result of a breeding between a white and mahogany native dog and a lemon and white dog brought to Brittany by an Englishman for the woodcock shooting. This pup became famous as a hunter and so everyone wanted to have his pups in turn.

But a French sportsman by the name of Arthur Enaud is given credit for the early development of the Brittany as it is known today. His idea was to intensify scenting ability and also breed for the orange and white color. He used for outcrosses, the Italian Bracco and the Braque de Bourbonnais, both pointing breeds. The latter had another desirable characteristic, a short tail. It had long been the custom of sportsmen in the Brittany region to dock, or cut short, the long tails of their dogs to keep them from being injured in the great fields of furze. So it was

very desirable to have naturally tail-less or short-tailed dogs.
In 1896 the first Brittany spaniel was shown in a dog show in
his native land. He was entered in the miscellaneous class because there was no regular class for the so-called "Short-tailed
Brittany."   In 1906 at a show in Toulouse the breed was given a
class of its own for the first time, a circumstance due entirely to
a railroad accident which prevented the sole Brittany entry from
being on time for the miscellaneous spaniel judging. Therefore,
it had to be judged alone. However, at a show in Nantes on May
31, 1907, the French Spaniel Club was founded and a committee
assigned to draw up a standard (desirable conformation points)
for the Brittany spaniel. This standard was presented to the then
newly organized Club de L'Epagneul Bretagne.

Again, just as it had gained them fame in their own land, it was
the hunting prowess of the Brittanys that first drew the interest
of Americans who travelled in France. Brittanys were first
brought here in 1931 and they soon began to make a dent. In 1934
the American Kennel Club granted the breed official recognition.
Sportsmen took the hard working little dogs to heart. The home
folk liked their looks and jaunty, endearing ways. Less than ten
years later, 1942 to be exact, there were enough enthusiasts
spread around the country to found the American Brittany Club.
Since their first appearance Brittanys have made a prominent
place for themselves in field trials, bench shows, and obedience
competition but, most of all, as an all-around pet which can, as the
saying goes, "double in brass."

To Be In The Pink

In order to be, and feel, in the pink of condition all dogs need exercise. It is up to you to create the kind of environment for your dog, whatever his breed, that gives him enough exercise of the right kind. Unfortunately there is a widespread, but thoroughly unfounded, belief that a dog needs complete freedom to get proper exercise. You will hear people say "I wouldn't have a dog in the city. Dogs should be where they can be free to run." There are dog owners in suburban and country areas who follow this same cult. These are the people who turn their dogs out in the morning and then forget about them for the rest of the day. Then they wonder why their dogs become "tramps," chase cars, get into fights with other dogs and, in general, form habits that make them neighborhood nuisances.

Dogs love human companionship far more than freedom to roam. They are strongly domesticated animals. Furthermore, a dog left to his own devices becomes less and less your own dog and you miss the chief joys of dog ownership. Your dog wants to belong to you, not to the universe. Isn't it true that the most intelligent and companionable dogs you've known are those which live closely with their owners as a member of the family?

A dog's habits are formed by his environment. He can't be a "smart" dog if he is shut up in the cellar, tied out to a post or left in a kennel yard day after day with no opportunity to learn

anything. He will be a dimwit through no fault of his own. Furthermore, he will feel unwanted and through frustration and idleness
come bad habits.

Your Brittany will not only learn by being with the family and
having attention, but he will get exercise by being taken on walks,
by romping with the children. Your puppy will exercise himself
in a number of ways. He chases butterflies, picks up a stick or a
shoe and parades around with it. It is easy to divert these natural
releases for his puppy energy to games that give him exercise.

Suppose you spend a little time each day throwing a ball for
your pup. He soon learns that if he brings it back, you will
throw it again. So he learns to retrieve. Suppose you take walks
with him. He learns how pleasant companionship is and stays at
your side. You talk to him and he soon learns his name and
many other words. When you put him out in the yard, make it a
point to speak to him occasionally. He won't be inclined to go
away from home, even if he is free, for fear he will miss some of
your charming conversation. Brittanys are not gregarious enough
to be natural roamers, but even a homebody will go elsewhere for
attention if he doesn't get it at home.

In the matter of climatic environment a Brittany is rugged and
fits into practically any category except possibly the frozen North
or equatorial Africa. It is a favorite breed for hunting in Mexico
where the temperature can soar to 80 degrees during the gunning
season. Many Brittanys are owned in New England and the Great
Lakes region and the majority have winter quarters in outdoor
kennels.

A Brittany spaniel is hardy enough to be quartered outdoors
provided he has a well-built doghouse, properly protected from
drafts and dampness. He should also have a yard with a strong
wire fence sufficiently high that he can't jump or climb over and
sunk deep enough into the ground so that he can't dig under it.
Even with a yard, however, he should have regular outside exercise such as play and daily walks with you and, when possible, an
occasional run in an open field. A city dog getting regular brisk
half-hour walks two or three times a day actually gets more exercise than a dog in a kennel yard. The latter often spends most of
his time lying in his bunk.

To be well nourished, dogs need certain essential nutritional
elements in their diet. They need protein, carbohydrates, miner-

als, fats and vitamins. In the days when the family table groaned under huge roasts and heaping dishes of various fare, the family pet made out fairly well on leftovers. Today's packaged foods and more restricted style of dining leave few table scraps. Besides, we know more about proper dog nutrition today and we have a number of excellent, prepared dog foods.

When you buy your pup, find out the kind of food he has been getting and use that, at least in the beginning. Sudden changes of food, or even types of milk, can cause temporary digestive upsets. However, don't make the mistake of sticking to such things as milk formulas and baby cereal after the pup has developed.

There is no trick to feeding dogs right. The best diet for your Brittany is a high quality prepared dog meal or kibble. To this you can add meat, preferably beef, good table scraps or canned dog food, or feed it plain, moistened with milk or meat broths. Horsemeat is put up in various ways for dogs and is widely used. Remember, however, that horsemeat is deficient in fat and some fat should be added when it is fed. Bacon drippings, melted lard or suet can be mixed in the meal or kibble (about a tablespoon to two capfuls of meal) and the whole moistened with water. Be sure when adding fat that it is fresh and not in the least rancid. Have the food lukewarm, never ice-cold from the refrigerator or hot.

Pork, corn, baked beans and cabbage-type vegetables are not usually digested well by dogs. Chicken or chop bones or any splintery type of bone should never be fed as they can damage the intestines. An occasional beef knuckle bone will be thoroughly enjoyed, but too much bone chewing wears down the teeth.

Specified amounts of food cannot always be followed for the reason that individual dogs differ in assimilating their food. The amount it takes to keep one dog sleek and firmly rounded may not be nearly enough for his own litter mate. So the question of "how much" is best answered by keeping an eye on your Brittany's figure. If he begins to have the contour of a balloon you are feeding too much; if he looks scrawny, feed more. As a guide consider that a grown Brittany needs about 1200 calories a day. A pound of prepared dog meal containing about nine percent fat, has approximately 1500 calories. A pound of canned dog food averages 450 calories. Because they are growing, puppies need more food than mature dogs. A Brittany that is working hard, such as during the hunting season, needs more food than the house pet.

Raising The Pup

The young puppy is making an abrupt change when he comes into a new home. He has never seen so many strange people before, never been the center of so much excitement and never been away from the familiar presence of his litter mates. Take all this into account when the new pup arrives and give him a chance to become acquainted gradually. In all probability the puppy is unaccustomed to children and their delighted shrieks and constant, possibly rough, handling upset and unnerve him. If he shows a desire to sit in a corner, respect his right to stay there undisturbed while he looks over his new situation, but speak to him and pet him occasionally. Your first job is to instill a feeling of confidence and security.

There are just a few things to remember in raising a puppy. He needs nourishing food and plenty of it, frequent rests and naps and lots of love. Your puppy has a natural confidence in you and this can be cultivated by never abusing this trust.

Some preparation must be made in advance for the puppy's arrival. Get a wood or heavy cardboard box; and, leaving three sides high enough to afford protection from drafts, cut the fourth side down just low enough for the pup to get in and out. Have it roomy enough so he can stretch out, and spread newspapers or an old blanket flat in the bottom. You can, of course, use a fancy basket or a dog crate; the purpose is the same—a resting place of

The "socialization" of puppies should begin early. By handling and cuddling for a little while each day, puppies learn to have confidence in human beings and are more easily adjusted and more trainable when they grow up.

his own where the pup will sleep and take his needed naps during the day. Keep his box in a permanent place where there is no draft nor direct heat from a radiator. Don't put it in a damp cellar. The best place is likely to be the kitchen or corner of the living

room where the pup can watch and hear the activities of the household when he is resting there.

Puppies, like growing boys, are always hungry and a good thing,
too, for to grow properly they must have plenty of nourishing food.
If they "go off" their feed for any length of time something is
wrong.

An important part of feeding puppies is to keep their meals on a
strict time schedule. Between the ages of six and ten weeks of

*Six-weeks old puppies (left) will be
on their own — even feet first in the
feed pan — if the weaning process is
started early.*

*The same puppies (right) at seven
weeks of age show better table manners! Competition at the feed pan
helps spur appetite.*

age a puppy should be fed four times a day at about four-hour
intervals. Then feed three times a day, morning, noon and evening,
until the pup is six months old; then you cut to two meals. Your
puppy may turn up his nose at one meal at an earlier age. If so,
dispense with it. After he is a year old, one meal a day is sufficient; although there is no harm in a morning snack. As you
decrease the number of meals, increase the amounts of food.

There is no need for "baby" foods or elaborately concocted
diets. Mix a good commercial dry meal with warmed milk for

Close-up of a three-week-old Brittany pup shows he's all ready for life's adventure.

the morning feeding; give broth or plain water for the noon and evening feedings, adding beef, lamb, or horsemeat cut in small pieces, or some canned dog food. An egg may be added daily or occasionally, but boil or otherwise cook it as raw egg white is not well digested by puppies. Once a day add a small teaspoonful of cod-liver oil or a concentrate halibut-liver oil with viosterol according to directions. This is important in winter when the puppy cannot get his "sunshine" vitamins straight. If your six-weeks-old puppy has been on a diet of baby food and milk when he comes to you, gradually add the commercial dry meal a little at a time, until it replaces the farina entirely.

For the kenneled puppy it is a good idea to keep the dry dog food available at all times in a hopper or plain pan. This gives the puppy something to nibble on, keeps him from being hungry if, for some reason, the regular feeding time is delayed. Fresh, clean water should be kept available in the kennel at all times. In the home, water can be given between meals. Don't feed between-meal snacks as they dull the pup's appetite and tend to make him a "fussy" eater. For the same reason, don't let your puppy dawdle over his meals. Take uneaten food away and don't feed again until the regular feeding time.

HOUSEBREAKING

This always seems to be the main concern of all new puppy owners, yet it is not nearly as much trouble as it has been built up to be. It is merely a matter of using good psychology instead of punishment. Housebreaking is the perfect example of preventive training. In other words, if the puppy is given ample opportunity to relieve himself in the right place, he will not get into the habit of doing it elsewhere. Most people make the mistake of allowing the puppy to have "accidents" and then use correction. This is a much longer and more odious process than taking time at the start to develop good habits.

A puppy has very little physical control until he is at least three months old. At six or eight weeks he has none and, moreover, he is not developed enough mentally to comprehend punishment for misdemeanors, especially those he cannot help. A puppy must relieve himself frequently during the first few weeks of his life; always after eating, after a nap, the first thing in the morning and the last at night. He will need several other opportunities, too, especially after exciting play. If he is always taken out at regular intervals (and this is where a rigid feeding schedule comes in handy), he will not be so likely to make mistakes. There will be some "accidents." No one yet has raised a puppy without them, but there will be many more if you give your pup the run of the house day and night. Instead, keep him within a child's play pen or improvise an enclosure using the low stiff wire edging used for protecting flower beds. Spread newspapers over the area. If you have a seldom-used room that might be the place to keep your puppy's box at night, covering the floor with paper.

The main reason for mistakes is that owners forget or neglect to take the puppy out regularly and let him wander about without being watched. Once he has made a mistake on a rug, blot it up with turkish toweling or a piece of blotting paper (this is very good to have handy when housebreaking) and wipe it with a solution of vinegar and water or one of the commercial products for removing stain. Puppy urine does not usually stain but these products also remove the odor which might encourage the puppy to use that spot again.

When he is free in the house keep an eye on the pup. When he begins to squat scoop him up and carry him outdoors. Always praise him extravagantly when he performs in the right place, and he will soon understand what you are trying to accomplish. Because a young pup must relieve himself so often, many people use the paper-breaking method. That is, instead of taking the puppy outdoors, they take him to a newspaper spread for that purpose some place in the house. This may be easier, especially if you live on the top floor of an apartment house, but it is not the best method for a Brittany. Also, there comes a time when you have to train him from paper to the outdoors. It is much more practical to do the training in one fell swoop. In a city apartment, don't put the pup on the rug while you get your hat in the morning or you will have a puddle. Get dressed first, then take the pup out of his bed or pen and carry him until you get him to the sidewalk.

Some people think that it is difficult to housebreak a kennel dog. It has been my experience that dogs which live in outdoor kennels most of the time are quite easily housebroken for the reason that they have never acquired the habit of using any place other than the ground, concrete yard or, perhaps, bare kennel floor.

If your puppy is kenneled outdoors, take him out for a run or some play and after he has had a good evacuation (and only then) bring him into your home. Let him nose around and learn what a house is. Then very soon take him outside again. Do this often and for gradually longer periods, always being watchful. In a short time the puppy will go to the door to be let out when he feels the urge to "go."

It is surprising how many otherwise intelligent people will tell you to "rub the puppy's nose in it." Don't do it. It doesn't teach the puppy anything except that the person he has learned to trust has done something that terrified and sickens him. It will not train him to be clean; neither will scolding nor chastising long after the deed is done. A puppy has a short memory. If the preventive process is faithfully carried out, your puppy will be housebroken so soon that you can brag about it.

Puppies should never have toys made with squeaking devices that might be swallowed or toys made of shreddable rubber. Hard rubber balls should be of pure latex rubber. The best toys are those made of leather or treated bone.

Your puppy will never be carsick if you take him for frequent short rides while he is young and hold him in your lap. Never take him for his first ride after he has just eaten. If he dislikes the movement of the car, get him used to sitting in the car while it is motionless.

Grooming The Brittany

The Brittany's coat requires no special care nor intricate trimming. However, in order that it will look its best and reflect the dog's inner good health it should be brushed every few days or at least every week. In the Fall the coat grows heavier, especially on dogs which are kenneled outdoors. At this time the dead hairs of the summer coat are shed. Shedding in the spring, when the winter coat drops out is usually more excessive.

You can help the process along by giving the coat daily attention. Take your dog outdoors or stand him on paper indoors and run both your hands down his back and sides from his neck to his tail. Then knead or massage his skin with your fingers and repeat the stroking. This will loosen and work out a surprising amount of hair that would otherwise drop out on your rugs and upholstery! Finish with a vigorous brushing, using a fairly stiff bristled brush. A coarse-toothed comb can be used for the feathering on the legs. The "furnishings," the longer hair on legs, rear, and underbody, are never profuse on the Brittany, but they do gather burrs in the field. Look for them and work them out. They often get entangled in hair close to the skin. While you're about it, look for ticks. They are bloodsucking parasites that attach themselves to the dog's skin. They are more prevalent in some areas than others, but are becoming increasingly widespread.

With the many preparations that are available today for removal and control of ticks, lice and fleas there is little excuse for a dog having any of these debilitating parasites. Keeping an eye out for fleas is part of good grooming practice. Get to work as soon as you find one and carry out the clean-up program to your dog's bedding or kennel as fleas breed in these places. During grooming look for signs of skin trouble. Have it treated before it gains headway. During treatment of any skin trouble keep grooming tools meticulously clean.

Look into your Brittany's ears occasionally. If they are filled with dirt and wax accumulation, take a piece of cotton on your finger, dip it in hydrogen peroxide, and clean them, using an outward motion so as not to push the dirt deeper. Never probe into the ear as you may do serious damage; that is only for the professional. If teeth are yellow with tartar formation, have your veterinarian remove it.

Although the toenails of well-exercised dogs are worn down naturally, you may at some time need a pair of regular dog clippers but use them cautiously so as not to injure the quick. Ordinary scissors won't do the job.

Hunting dogs' eyes often become irritated and scratched from briars and weeds. Use any eyewash meant for human use. A good practice is to carry a small tube of one percent yellow oxide of mercury in your hunting coat pocket. Squeeze some into your Brittany's eyes when you come in from the fields. It will heal scratches and prevent infection.

When you give your Brittany a bath, rinse thoroughly. Most dandruff is caused by haphazard rinsing. If your dog's skin is dry and full of dandruff, add more fat to the diet, give more exercise, and use a skin lotion.

Ten to one if you follow the practice of brushing his coat, your Brittany will seldom need a bath. The same holds true if his life is largely outdoors (unless he rolls in cow manure as most dogs will). The brush and undergrowth through which he runs automatically cleans his coat. If your Brittany has a "doggy" odor, find the cause. It may be simply that his bedding needs changing. Smelly bedding makes a smelly dog. Ear canker, anal gland trouble, bad teeth, mange, and worm infestation are causes of bad odor. There is nothing offensive about the natural smell of a clean healthy dog.

Grooming your Brittany for showing is nothing more than having him clean (do not bathe just before a show as it may make his coat too fluffy) and snipping a little here and there to emphasize certain features. The long single hairs that sprout from eyebrows and muzzle should be clipped short.

The Brittany requires almost no grooming but a daily brushing and inspection of the coat is good health insurance. Moreover, it "feels good."

Basic Training

Every dog must have some degree of training. Whatever your ultimate goal for your Brittany—house pet, field companion or show dog; or, as with many Brittany owners, all three—basic training is the same.

Give your pup a name and use it often so that he learns to respond to it. Call him by name to his meals. When he is playing in the yard call him to you occasionally. He will come more readily if you stoop low to the ground. Always give him a warm welcome and he will soon learn to come when called. Never call your dog to you for scolding or disciplining. Always go to him under such circumstances.

When the pup finds something else too diverting to come to your call, attach a long, light rope to his collar. Let him drag this around the yard. If he ignores your call to come, pick up the end of the rope and pull him in steadily. Repeat this lesson at various times, never overlong, until he learns that he must obey.

Teach him the word "No" early by using it whenever you take something away from him that you don't want him to have or lead him away from some place you don't want him to be. You can teach him to "sit" on command by pressing down on his hind-quarters with one hand, rewarding him with a tidbit with the other.

In all training be consistent. Don't permit your pup to lie on a chair one day and then scold him the next time you find him there.

Manners apply in the kennel as well as in the home. The command "stay back" has many uses and in the kennel keeps the dog from bounding out whenever the gate is opened.

If you encourage him to jump up on you when you have on dungarees, don't blame him if he does the same when you are dressed to go to a party. When he jumps up take his feet in your hands, place them on the ground, repeating firmly "down," while you pet him approvingly. All training is basically showing approval and disapproval. A dog wants to please. Brittanys are usually sensitive and roughness in training often only defeats your purpose.

A kenneled pup may bark at night or other times. If he is in with another dog or pup, make sure the latter is not lying in the doorway and forcing the pup to stay out in the cold. If he is kenneled alone and you know he is fed and comfortable, go out and command him to be "quiet" at the same time giving him a dash of water from a water pistol or pail. The water cure is surefire but must be carried out consistently. Your dog will learn to stop merely on command alone.

There is nothing that loses your neighbor's good will like having your dog howl or bark continuously when he is left alone in the house.

Training a dog to stay alone without raising a rumpus is simply a matter of showing the puppy that he can't always have human companionship. Brittanys are not inclined to be noisy and usually meet any situation with calm acceptance . . . but there can be exceptions to all rules. In any case, most dogs that bark or chew up the draperies when they are left alone have been accustomed to having someone with them all the time. So start the puppy right. Put him in his box, or in another room with a favorite toy, for short periods during the day. As he grows up he learns to accept such separations. In nice weather he can be put outside in his kennel yard. If he cries, pay no attention. He'll soon settle down. When he has been "good" for an appreciable length of time, let him out and praise him. This procedure teaches two things . . . that being alone isn't a catastrophe and that someone always returns to him. Putting the pup in the car while it is standing in your driveway, and letting him take a nap on the seat perhaps will teach him to stay there quietly at times when you leave him in the car elsewhere while you market or shop. Whenever you leave your Brittany in an automobile make doubly sure that at least one window is partially open—especially on hot summer days.

Chasing cars, bicycles or passers-by is another habit that is

"Oh, so comfortable! Do I have to get down?" It's all right if you don't mind but be fair . . .

easily discouraged in the young puppy, hard to break in a grown dog. Always keep your eye on your pup when he's out in an unfenced yard. If he shows interest in running after a vehicle, call "no" sharply, then call him in to you. If he is persistent, keep a long, lightweight rope attached to his collar. Grab the end and stop him by force with a jerk to remind him to obey. Sometimes having someone stationed on the other side of a hedge or somewhere else nearby armed with loops of chain or empty tin cans fastened together which are thrown towards the dog when he starts out of the yard will teach him to stay away from this "danger." The trusty water pistol comes in handy in this training, too.

The word "No" should not be used carelessly for every little puppy prank. Use it only when you mean it and as the dog is starting to do something wrong not after he is in the process. At that time use the word "stop" in a sharp tone and, again, don't use it for trivial matters, only for important ones and then see to it that he does stop. Fox example, jumping, however lovingly, on a small frightened child, or bristling at another dog. But never forget to give those words of praise and show of approval when he does desist with a "no" or "stop."

Training For The Hunt

Start early to encourage your Brittany to hunt. Take him for walks in rough fields where he is likely to find a game bird or rabbit. Let him roam around. If he sticks close to your side at first, don't be discouraged; and if possible, take him with another hunting dog. After he has learned to get out and hunt, carry a blank pistol or lightly-loaded small bore gun. When he is at a good distance from you, chasing a sparrow or absorbed in some enticing scent, shoot the gun. He may stop and look. Pay no attention and keep going as if nothing happened. Shoot seldom and at gradually decreased distances. Never shoot a gun near a young dog to "see if he is gun shy" or he will surely become so. Rattling pans just before you put down his feed is another way to get a puppy to associate noise with something pleasant.

Although your Brittany will eventually point the scent of game, much can be done to encourage sight-pointing in the young pup. To the end of a fishing rod attach a string about four feet long. Tie a piece of paper or cloth to the end and twitch this across the ground to attract the pup's attention. He will probably stalk it and try to catch it but you snatch it out of his reach. When he finds he can't catch it he will probably stiffen up into a point when the object is held stationary. After he begins to point have someone else handle the rod and when your pup points go up to him and stroke him gently, repeating the word "whoa" so that

A sight to thrill any sportsman. A dog on point with three in the background honoring the point. Demonstrated here are the finished manners on game that make the members of this foursome leading contenders in field trials.

he will associate the word with pointing staunchly. Use the same method when the pup sight-points a robin on the lawn or a barnyard chicken. "Whoa" is the bird-dog trainer's greatest asset, but it must be used with discrimination and only when the pup is on point, not when he is ignoring the word and heartily chasing a bird. There is much more to field training than can be covered here, but you will be off to the right start. Never prolong any training lesson until the pup is tired or bored and do not expect too much. Serious training should not begin until the pup is at least six months old.

The term "serious training" should probably be explained. All training is serious to the degree that it is a combination in the right proportions of encouraging and discouraging the dog's natural instincts. It is instinctive for a pup to hesitate or point momentarily, either sight-pointing a bird on the ground (like the paper at the end of the fishing rod line) or the scent of game. It is also instinctive for him to chase the bird if it runs or is flushed into the air. We encourage pointing. Eventually we will discourage chasing but if restraint is put on a young pup in this regard we also discourage his desire to hunt and his boldness on game. Restricting, or worse still, disciplining a young dog before he has acquired a keen love of hunting and familiarity with game may make him bird-shy, or, at best, completely disinterested in the work he was meant to do.

Dogs are not machines. They are distinctly individuals so the manner of training must also be adapted to the temperament of your pupil. You must understand your dog. The way of handling an aggressive dog will not do for the more sensitive type. Some dogs are quicker to learn, others develop more slowly. Intuition plays a strong part in your success as a trainer. You must understand your dog and, of course, gain his confidence.

There is one important lesson that the trainer himself must learn . . . self control. One ill-timed burst of temper can undo long hours, even days, of training. Moreover, the dog's confidence in his trainer can be ruined. Certainly, it's discouraging to have a dog completely disregard something you think he has learned but you must accept such occurrences as only natural. When you begin to feel frustrated or angry, knock off for the time being. Put your dog in his kennel or the house and go do something else for awhile.

There are times when a dog goes stale on his training. Then it's best to give him a rest for a few days. Always, in any lesson, stop when the dog has accomplished something. Then you both end on a happy refrain and not a sour note. In other words, make your training sessions short and sweet . . . don't prolong them even though the dog is doing well.

If you want your Brittany to retrieve, start it as a game when he is young. Make a runway by putting a low wire fence about four feet out from the side of a building or wall. Make it about fifteen to twenty feet in length and enclosed at one end. When you take your pup out to play, have a burlap-wrapped "dummy" or a dead pigeon. Get the pup's attention by showing it to him invitingly, then throw it to the end of the enclosure. He will probably go

Brittany Spaniels—one on point, the other "backing" or honoring the point — stay steady while gunner walks in to flush a covey.

after it and pick it up. Then call him to you. The fence prevents his running off in any other direction except straight towards you at its open end so he gets into the habit of retrieving to you promptly. Take the "bird" and throw it again. But repeat it only a couple of times.

If he doesn't pick it up or only brings it part way, pick it up yourself, tease him with it a bit and throw it a shorter distance. After he has made a couple of retrieves, stop. He will be eager to continue the "game" and perhaps do even better the next day. Prolonging a lesson or making a pup repeat something he has learned over and over, will tire and bore him and may very well undo all that has been accomplished.   All lessons should be given when there are no distracting elements such as other dogs or people.   Young dogs are easily diverted or confused by too much going on around them.

For the same reason when you first take your dog hunting, don't have a half dozen other hunters along. Go alone or with a companion who is both sympathetic with the fact that you are initiating a young dog and a good shot. Game killed neatly is a great inducement in encouraging your dog to hunt and teaching him what it is all about.   There is nothing like experience to make a good gun dog.   If you live in an area where game is plentiful, you are fortunate.   If you don't, there are a great many places where you can go to hunt for a price—the commercial game farms where you pay for the number of birds you want released and then go out and hunt them.

Such places are also useful when the time comes for training your dog to be staunch and steady on game. You can "plant" birds for your dog to find.   You can, of course, also use pigeons or guinea hens.   But don't overdo work on planted birds or you will make a mechanical dog or perhaps even "sour" him on game.   Never use hobbled or tied birds at any time.

You want your dog to be staunch on point . . . that is, stay there until you can walk up and flush the birds or bird. Attach a lightweight cord to his collar, about 20-30 feet long. Let it drag. When he points or nears game, pick up the end of the cord and walk slowly up to him saying "whoa" in a low tone of voice. Then stroke him gently down his back from shoulders to tail, continuing to say "whoa" softly.   Have a companion flush the game.   Your dog will probably chase. Let him. You are now working on staunchness, not steadiness to flush.

Handling your dog on point has many advantages. It gives him confidence in what he is doing. He knows he is pleasing you and when you are calm he is encouraged to stay in that position. Sometimes a dog becomes excited when you approach and will run in and flush. So go in from the side at first. Don't rush up; even

Praise for a good delivery of a game bird will encourage prompt and quick retrieving.

stop occasionally as you speak to him. After he becomes accustomed to your approach, vary the direction, coming from the other side or from behind. As time goes on you can increase your pace, eventually even approaching on a run.

As he gains experience and age you will want him to be steady to the flush. That is when you apply force. You repeat the same action of stroking but keep a firm grip on the cord and when he starts to chase call "whoa" and hold tight. He'll be jerked to a stop, perhaps head over heels. Draw him to you by the cord, stand him in the place he started from and keep him there, walking around him, repeating "whoa."

All these things do not happen in just that order, or in a few months time. Remember that there must first be instilled a love of hunting. Study your pupil. If he becomes uneasy or confused, let up on pressure and permit him to have fun again. However, you must try to judge the right times to let up and bear down. Actually, Brittanys are not inclined to be hard headed so you should have little trouble if you just apply good common sense.

Field trials are an interesting, sporting pursuit. If you go to a few you will probably be bitten by the bug. Field trials are outdoor events in which dogs are given the opportunity to show their ability in the field in competition with other dogs. Conditions are those of actual hunting except that game birds, either pheasants or quail, are usually liberated or "planted" in the area, so that every dog will have an opportunity on birds. The dogs entered are run in braces, and are competing against each other and against every other dog in the stake. Each brace runs a specified time or "heat" which may be from twenty minutes for puppies to a half hour or an hour for other stakes.

There are amateur handler stakes and many amateurs become so adept that they train and handle their own dogs. Others, particularly those who have neither time nor ability or the facilities to do their own training, place their dogs with a professional trainer . . . either for training as a gun dog, and, or field trail competition. There are a number of trainers who specialize in Brittanys.

To show that purebred dogs have brains as well as beauty, obedience trials have become a popular feature of dog shows. The dogs are scored solely on how well they carry out a prescribed set of exercises. A dog's score can give him credit toward an obedience degree, C.D., C.D.X., and U.D. (Companion Dog, Companion

When the young dog points, the use of a check cord will keep him from rushing in and help in teaching him to be steady on point.

Dog Excellent and Utility Dog). When won the degree is permanently noted after the dog's name. Many Brittanys have competed successfully in obedience trials, the training for which is carried out in obedience training classes throughout the country.

These training classes are sponsored by a training club or group with the purpose of teaching the owner how to train and handle his own dog. A listing of clubs in the various areas of the country can be obtained, free, upon request, from the Gaines Dog Research Center, 250 Park Ave., New York 17, N.Y.

The owner or some member of the family takes the dog to the classes. The age at which dogs are admitted is usually eight months, although some groups permit dogs of six months to start. There is usually a Beginners' Course, with all the exercises done on leash. They include "heeling" which is to have your Brittany stay at your left side, walking there without pulling ahead, while

"Down!" Spoken sharply with a thrust of the knee will teach the dog not to jump up on people. Once learned, the command alone is sufficient.

In teaching the dog to "heel," hold leash short, pull him back to position and use the word "heel" when he pulls ahead. Swinging the other end of the leash in front of his nose helps to get across the idea.

you hold the leash with the right hand, guided through your left. "Sit" or sitting at command—this done by a taut hold on the leash to keep the dog's head up while you press down on his hindquarters, coming when called and going to heel position, standing at heel, sitting and "staying" there are other exercises learned by beginners.   The Novice Course is the next step, with heeling to include walking in a Figure 8 with your dog at your side, some exercises off leash—that is, without having the leash attached to the dog's collar—and "drop" or to have the dog lie down at a hand signal.   An Intermediate Course is usually a review of previously learned exercises plus carrying and retrieving articles. The Open and Utility Courses carry further and add refinements to the basic lessons learned in the first classes.

Each course is usually for a period of nine to ten weeks at a nominal fee, with from one and a half to two and a half hours of training a week with graduation exercises after completing the course.   Although many persons who attend such classes become interested in Obedience competition in dog shows, others simply profit by the experience in making their dogs nicely behaved and more manageable at home.

It may be that you will have to rely on your own efforts in training your Brittany.   Well, you have taught him to come when called by encouraging him to do so when he was a pup. He "sits" when you tell him to, for the same reason. With this as a start you have the basic "do's" and since your pup also understands the meaning of the word "no" you have the basic "don'ts." These few commands with variations, can be applied to fit almost any case. For example suppose you are walking with your dog and he sees a cat, another dog or something else for which he jumps and pulls hard on the leash.   A sharp jerk on your end of the leash and a "no" will show him that you want him to mind his own business. "Sit" has an infinite number of uses. It can be used to advantage in a car, not only to keep your dog from getting the habit of bounding about while you're driving, but if you make him sit while you get out of the car and have him stay there until you tell him "all right," it will prevent him from scrambling to jump out of the car ahead of everyone else the minute the car is stopped. The uses of coming when called are likewise of endless use.

A good rule around the house is to have your dog learn "place." This should be a location where he won't be in anybody's way. It

"Well, I've done it and maybe I'll go all the way," the pupil seems to say. But with repetition, encouragement and lots of praise, he will soon associate the word "sit" with the act.

To teach the dog to "sit" at command, press down on his flanks while holding up his head by means of the leash.

should also be some place that he likes. Perhaps he has chosen one, under a desk or table or in a corner of a room. Put his mattress or pillow there. Call him, point to it and say "place." If he doesn't get the idea right away, put him in position, press gently on his shoulders with your left hand and pull his front legs forward with your right hand so he will be lying down. Repeat the command and hold him in position for a few moments. Then, repeating the word, lift your right hand slowly and hold it just above his head. Then you add "stay" pronouncing it clearly.

You are most likely to have success if you choose a time after your pup has eaten and had a walk or romp. The final step is to send him to his "place" by giving the command and pointing to the spot. If necessary, go with him or take him there time after time. After a week if you can send him to his place from across the room you have practically won. You must always be sure to praise and pet him as soon as he gives the first indication of understanding your desire. "Place" is a good thing for your dog to know. It will keep your Brittany from underfoot when you have

A young dog learns to accept the leash more readily if the handler encourages him by running a little and making it a "fun" game.

Budding sportsman. . .this young fellow knows that a good dog and safe gun handling is the right combination for pleasure in the field and good hunting.

a room full of guests, or when you are cooking a holiday dinner. When your dog goes to his place of his own accord, his wishes to be undisturbed should be respected.

Whatever the form of training, whether for the home, the car or the field, remember that it is not a matter of getting a precise result in a definite way. You have to figure out your own individual dog. One can never say "If you do this, your dog will do exactly thus and so." You have to make allowances for age, for puppy antics, certain circumstances and individual traits. But once a lesson has been learned, make sure that you get obedience. If you give a command, give it for good reason and not just any old time for trivialities, and then make sure that it's obeyed, even if only in token form.   This doesn't mean severity or punishment. It just means that you must be consistent and take the time then and there to put over the idea that you mean it. And never forget that praise and approval at the right time is the keyword in training.   The Brittany has a willing spirit and will always respond cheerfully and with zest.

Showing Your Brittany

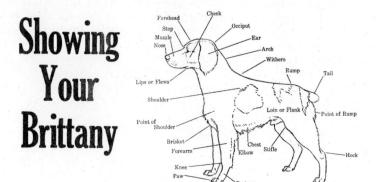

Showing your Brittany can mean a whole new world of exciting experiences and new friends with common interests. But first, go to a dog show. Watch the judging and the procedure in the ring. Don't let it confuse you. A dog show is simply an elimination contest which proceeds in orderly fashion until one dog stands alone as "Best-in-Show." First is the breed competition. The best of each breed enters the group competition. There are six groups: Sporting (which is the Brittany's group), Hound, Working, Terrier, Toy and Non-Sporting. The dog selected as the winner of its particular group then competes for Best-in-Show, so that it boils down to six dogs which appear in the final judging.

If your dog has never seen anyone else but your own family group, never heard the rumble of a train or the backfire of a truck, don't expect him to strut proudly into his first show ring. He may. Some dogs are born with such assurance, but he is more likely to collapse like a soft-boiled egg. So, before you enter your Brittany in a show accustom him to the confusion and crowds he will meet there. Take him among people for walks on busy thoroughfares.

Practice walking him on a light show leash or "lead," as it is called, in your yard. Encourage him by tidbits and praise to keep up his naturally brisk pace. Try to keep him on your left side which is the show position while "gaiting" or "moving" a dog in the ring.   Pose him so that he is standing squarely on all four feet, with leash off, holding his jaw with one hand and the tip of his tail with the other. Use a tidbit to train him to "stay." Find a way to attract his attention with a tidbit, squeaking device or whispering his pet name to induce him to lift his ears in that typical Brittany expression.   When he has learned to stay in position, have someone, preferably a stranger "go over him" as a judge will do in the ring, running his hands over the back and pressing firmly but not heavily on the hindquarters. All this won't be accomplished in one day, of course, but a little at a time.

You may hear of a sanctioned match show being held in your community. That is a good place to begin. Match shows are informal events in which you can enter your dog on the day of the show and where you will find many other novices in the same boat as you are. Don't worry if your dog acts either like a hoodlum or a shrinking violet. No one expects beginners to be perfect. A handler can do a number of things to show off a dog to best advantage and the "personality" dog with a sense of showmanship often has an advantage, but the basis of judging is your dog's physical beauty and structural soundness in conformance with the standard for the breed. Be confident and you will transmit that feeling to your dog. Forget about yourself. The judge is looking at your dog, not you; so always keep your dog between yourself and the judge. Puppy matches are sometimes held where there are classes for puppies from two to nine months. Puppies must be at least six months old to be entered in the regulation championship point shows. A match show when available is a good place to gain experience for greater things to come, for you will no sooner win your first ribbon in a match than you will be thinking of more important competition.

All shows are held under the rules of the American Kennel Club and its monthly magazine, *Pure-Bred Dogs*, lists all coming shows. Find a convenient show and write to the secretary or the superintendent for a premium list. This contains the entry form and all the information about the show. The regular classes are: Puppy, Novice, Bred by Exhibitor, American Bred and Open (you will probably enter Puppy or Novice). Return the entry form with the fee.   There are benched and unbenched shows, the latter usually held in the summer. At a bench show platforms are provided with separated compartments for each dog and this is where your dog will stay except when in the ring or being exercised.

At most shows, and always at indoor shows, "exercise" pens are provided in some out-of-the-way corner—one for females, one for males. These are enclosed areas, spread with shavings, for dogs to be put into to run about and relieve themselves. It is not charged against your dog if he has to heed nature's call in the ring, or aisles, but it's much nicer if these things are taken care of beforehand. Your dog will be more comfortable and better able to keep his mind on his work, and it will save you embarrassment if he is well emptied out so that he isn't "obligated" in the ring.

For the same reason, it is wise to feed lightly, if at all, on the day of a show, or any other occasion where your dog will be on exhibition, such as a field trial or obedience trial. Give enough water to satisfy thirst rather than keeping it available so that he may drink more than necessary. Hot weather makes a difference, of course. Be sure your Brittany gets a good run or walk, on the morning of a show, to relieve himself and so be more comfortable traveling and during the show.

When you leave your dog on his bench, be sure he is chained short enough so that he can't jump off and hang, strangling, halfway over the edge. These suggestions may seem of minor importance but they are good to know from the start, and many a veteran exhibitor regrets that he had to learn them by hard experience.

About a week before the show you will receive a receipt for your entry and a judging schedule. Get your equipment ready, a bench chain with snaps at each end to use on the bench—you have your lightweight lead. Of course, you have your Brittany shining, but take along some grooming tools for a last minute brush-up, a turkish towel, a mat or rug for his bench, a thermos of water and drinking dish. You may think you need some aspirin for yourself. You won't, you'll have fun!

In each of the five regular classes the judge awards ribbons for first, second, third and fourth prizes. The sexes are judged separately. The first prize winners in the male classes compete for Winners' Dog. After he is selected the others compete for Reserve Winners. The same procedure is repeated in judging the females. Winners' Dog and Winners' Bitch then compete for Best of Winners. He or she is then matched against champions of both sexes entered in the Specials Class and the judge selects

Best of Breed. Dogs of the opposite sex to the Best of Breed who competed in the Best of Winners and Best of Breed then compete for Best of Opposite Sex.

How does a champion get that way? Points, the number of which is determined by the number of competitors of its breed and sex in regular classes, are given to each Winners' Dog and Winners' Bitch. To become a champion a dog or bitch must win fifteen points under at least three judges. At least two of the shows must rate as three-point shows or larger. In other words, to be a champion a dog must prove his merit in the eyes of at least three judges in three or more shows and at least two of the shows must provide higher than average competition.

Care Of Your Brittany

Since the Brittany is a hard working tenacious hunter, he has his share of mishaps in the field. Because he is such a valiant worker, he will continue the hunt on three legs if necessary. Therefore it behooves you, the handler, to know what to do to prevent mishaps as well as how to care for your dog in general. The intelligent owner should know his own limitations in handling ailments. He should know when to seek the help of one who knows more—his veterinarian.

Let us consider first the general care of the Brittany—care that will help to keep him healthy, hearty and happy. This is no more than the application of a little common sense—that sense which people often fail to apply to themselves. Look your dog over as often as necessary with a critical eye for trouble, particularly after a trip to the field. Check his eyes for particles of bark, etc., and if necessary flush the eyes with warm water. Examine the nose and ear flaps for abrasions which when found may be swabbed with an antiseptic such as tincture of iodine. Run your hands over his body to find skin abrasions, burrs, snarls, etc., and if they are a problem in your area check for ticks at this time. Last, but not least, check his feet, his pads and nails for difficulties. This examination should take perhaps sixty seconds and may save many future headaches. Other than after a run, you should examine your dog at regular intervals for developments which can and do occur in all dogs. Examine the ears; they should be clean and of a healthy pink color. If they are otherwise, smell them for the telltale sour odor of ear canker. For help with this and the following maladies, consult your veterinarian. Examine those important organs—the teeth. If they appear stained, they may need to have tartar removed. The gums should be a healthy pink color and with healthy teeth and gums, you will note his breath is not offensive. The coat of the Brittany is "a thing of beauty." If dull and lifeless, all is not well. It is simple to discover the presence of fleas, lice and ticks and when found, they should be eliminated. Motheaten-like areas on the head and front of the front legs should not be passed off as briar or cat scratches. Have them examined by a professional.

The two anal glands located on either side and slightly below the center of the anus may give your dog trouble. An indication of difficulty here may be the dog's dragging himself along in a sitting position with rear legs extended. This symptom is one sign that the glands should be emptied. Occasionally, one of the anal glands may swell and rupture. This is an exceedingly painful condition and requires treatment.

In addition to the general considerations, let us consider the prevention of infectious diseases. In this case your veterinarian will tell you the proper method of vaccination for the prevention of distemper, infectious canine hepatitis, rabies and leptospirosis. In some areas, veterinarians do not recommend preventative inoculations for all four of these diseases.

Let's consider each disease separately. Canine distemper is *the* great killer of dogs. It has been said more dogs die of distemper every year in this country than from all other infectious diseases together. This virus is transmitted by direct contact as well as being airborne. The incubation period is between six and nine days. Fever with depression is the first symptom. This is followed by improvement in spirits and lower fever for a day about three days after the onset. From then on the fever again becomes elevated for a week or more. This second rise of temperature may be accompanied by cough, nasal and optic discharges, diarrhea and even pneumonia.

If treatment is started early, chances for recovery are better. Not infrequently, in spite of treatment, nervous symptoms develop such as chorea (twitching) and convulsions or both. When we consider that all the horrors of distemper as well as the expense of treatment involved can be prevented by a few injections it is well worth the effort and cost to provide them.

Another important disease is infectious canine hepatitis. This virus has been understood for a relatively short time. It is much more serious to dogs under a year of age than to older dogs. Often a non-productive cough with or without tonsillitis is an early symptom. Tests indicate that fifty percent of all dogs over one year of age have had this disease. Since only ten percent of those which develop infectious hepatitis show symptoms it is obviously not as serious as is distemper. Also with this in mind, it may be understood why many veterinarians are not too insistent that all pups have inoculations. It is my opinion that puppies which are apt to have contact with large numbers of stray dogs or neighborhood dogs should be given protection. The inoculations do not make the puppy a carrier. Injections are usually given in two parts seven to ten days apart and should be repeated every six to twelve months. A new combination of distemper virus and hepititis vaccine given in one injection shows promise. Recovered adult dogs and puppies may be carriers for nine months or perhaps longer. There is also a serum injection which confers a ten to twenty-one day immunity.

Rabies is the most important virus disease of the dog insofar as man is concerned. It is incurable in both man and beast. If your Brittany is used in the field where rabies is reported, even though rarely, he should be inoculated according to your state's regulations. The World Health Organization and some states recognize one injection of chick embryo rabies virus for three years. Your veterinarian will tell you about the advisability of protection for your dog. This disease usually follows a bite from another animal. The first symptoms are often personality changes ranging from unusual affection to belligerency and hiding in dark places. This is followed in one to three days by aggressiveness toward moving objects, whether it be the hand or any object moving before the affected animal. Death usually occurs a few days after nervous symptoms are displayed.

Canine leptospirosis is a bacterial disease and is divided into two types—canicola fever which is spread through urine from dog to dog and is the more prevalent of the two. The second type which causes infectious jaundice is transmitted through the urine of rodents, especially rats. The incubation period is from five to fifteen days. It causes a varying elevation of temperature with loss of appetite, often ulcers in the mouth, and finally depression and death in fifty percent of the untreated dogs aflicted, five to ten days after the onset. Although both types run similar courses, infectious jaundice as the name suggests, causes jaundice or yellowing of the membranes of the body. There is a preventive inoculation for this disease. If for no other reason than to keep infectious jaundice down to a minimum, the rat population of an area should be destroyed. If treatment is started early enough, it is usually successful.

In view of recent laboratory advancements in virus culture which have brought to light over 100 new human viruses in 1955 and 1956, it is expected that many viruses which are affecting our dogs will be isolated in the next few years.

The Brittany has his share of the internal parasites; the four major ones being roundworms, hookworms, whipworms and tapeworms. Roundworms are usually important only in puppies up to one year of age. These are the five to six-inch worms about the shape of an earthworm. They are white to pink in color and coil up like a spring when first expelled. The roundworms as well as the hookworms have part of their life cycle in the blood stream, lungs and intestinal tract.

The hookworm is about three-quarters of an inch long and almost as thin as a human hair. It is virtually never seen in a stool, but the telltale eggs may be seen under your veterinarian's microscope. The whipworm is not found in young dogs as often as in those one year of age or older. This is perhaps the most difficult common internal parasite to control, since the eggs have been found to live for over five years in the soil. With the roundworms, hookworms and whipworms, a routine stool check by your veterinarian will enable him to find any worm eggs present and to recommend to you the method for keeping these pests down to a minimum or to remove them entirely. A symptom of hookworm as well as roundworm infestations may be a dry cough but since a cough may be a symptom of more serious conditions, ask your veterinarian's advice.

The tapeworm is a common pest in the Brittany and is usually carried to the dog by fleas. While the adult worm is about eighteen inches long, only the last segment is seen on the stool or clinging to the hair around the anus. Often motile, the segment stretches and shrinks sometimes moving one end back and forth in "cobra fashion." These segments are about one-quarter to one-half inch when first passed, but then dry, contracting to much smaller tan, seed-like objects which also cling to the hair around the anus. Although not the usual cause, these segments may at times prompt a dog to drag his rear end along the ground.

Although internal parasites alone may cause diarrhea in your Brittany, this condition is more often caused by bacterial or protozoan infections. For any of these conditions, your veterinarian is the man to see.

Another parasite which may plague your Brittany is the heartworm. The adult worms live in the blood of the heart or in the great vessels of the heart. This parasite is transmitted by the bite of a blood-sucking insect such as the flea and mosquito. Tiny "wigglers" or immature worms from an affected animal are passed by such a bite from an insect which has dined previously on such an animal. It requires nine months for the adult heartworms to mature and reproduce. Until the adults reproduce, this pest cannot be diagnosed since the test demands that immature worms be found under the microscope in a sample of blood. Although a more serious pest in the southeastern United States, this disease has been found in all states of the Union. The treatment should be given by a veterinarian and often must be repeated several times to be effective. In older dogs, the treatment may be too much for the dog, resulting in death.

Of the external parasites, perhaps follicular or "red" mange has been most troublesome over the years. This microscopic cigar-shaped mite should be no great problem with the remedies available in this day and age. First let us consider what the disease looks like. It usually, but not always, becomes noticeable on one of two areas of the body—the head or the front legs. The affected areas appear "moth-eaten" in the early stages and not very significant. As time passes (sometimes weeks) the disease may break out anywhere over the body, often causing intense itching with subsequent scratching and biting. It is after scratching that the affected areas become red—thus the name "red" mange. Since foxes and other wild animals may and often do carry follicular mange, our Brittany spaniels can contract the disease afield and not necessarily from direct contact. Prevention is difficult if not impossible; however, early diagnosis and treatment will assure an early cure in most cases. Your veterinarian should be consulted for diagnosis and treatment.

Sarcoptic mange is caused by a crablike parasite which lives and reproduces under the skin. Like follicular mange it causes itching and reddening of the skin. However, it is more easily cured than the former, a host of home remedies being effective.

Other skin diseases are perhaps not as common with Brittany spaniels as with many breeds; however, seasonal skin diseases are not rare. Keep the coat clean by providing clean kennel space or other housing and by bathing only when necessary. Bathing with soap and water removes natural oil from the skin, thus predisposing the dog to summer skin diseases. Many commercial dry baths and dry cleaners are available for your dog which are helpful in place of a soap and water bath. These preparations are useful in keeping the flea population down. Fleas seem to be important in spreading skin diseases since once an infection starts, fleas biting the dog in the infected area may carry the disease to a non-infected area.

If a soap and water bath is necessary, use a mild hand soap and follow it with a flea-killing rinse. This technique will also control lice, but should be repeated in ten days to destroy the newly-hatched eggs or nits which the first bath did not kill. Ticks are a problem with Brittanys as with any bird dog breed. Commercial tick powders and solutions are effective. Your veterinarian can help with this problem. If ticks are to be removed by force, always twist them or use a freshly-extinguished match head. Touching a tick while the match is still hot will cause him to back out. Gasoline and turpentine have the same effect; keep these off the skin.

Of all skin afflictions, perhaps the most difficult is the non-parasitic summer condition often called summer eczema. As the name implies the disease occurs in summer months causing itching, usually starting on the back above the base of the tail and spreading up the back. Often hair falls out in varying degrees. With the hair loss, inflamed skin is visible. Since this is a difficult problem consult your veterinarian. In some cases a fungicidal powder is useful as a preventative and may be combined with a flea powder.

Not unusual is an infection of the outside of the lower lips just behind the position of the upper canine teeth when the jaw is closed. This is an extremely persistent infection due to the fact that a seepage of saliva may keep the area moist allowing bacteria to flourish which could not if the area were kept dry. Ointments massaged into the areas are effective and your veterinarian will provide the proper treatment.

A Brittany's feet are all important and must be kept in running shape. If your dog does not exercise enough to wear his nails down then you must cut them as necessary. Cut them little and often—not short and infrequently as a short cut may cause pain and bleeding.

Rashes which may hinder the dog's performance do occur between the pads of the feet and should be treated in the early stages.

Another difficulty in the Brittany as with any dog is constipation. This condition is easily prevented by proper diet and when present in the otherwise healthy animal is almost invariably caused by eating bones. An occasional beef rib bone will clean the teeth but other than that they are a useless ingredient in the diet. Constipation is easily recognized by persistent unsuccessful attempts at stooling. Sometimes several tablespoonfuls of mineral oil fed to the dog will help as will adult glycerine suppositories inserted rectally. If these do not work in six hours, let your veterinarian handle the problem.

A problem which must *not* be treated lightly is that of convulsions. They may be caused by improper feeding or by worms, neither of which are too serious. Epilepsy which is not well understood as well as infectious diseases may also cause convulsions. The first two causes are easily corrected, the third may be helped, and the last is usually fatal.

Still another condition which is often serious is a nasal infection. It may be caused by virus diseases or bacterial infections. In either case this symptom should be a signal for immediate action.

In this day and age of new chemicals for killing pests, there are more and more opportunities for your dog to be poisoned. Some poisons are almost invariably fatal—even when treated minutes after ingestion. Food and garbage poisoning is also a serious menace. If you are aware of such poisoning and cannot get immediate treatment for your dog, give an adult three ounces of three percent hydrogen peroxide with three ounces of water and a proportionately smaller quantity to a puppy. This will cause an emptying of the stomach in a few minutes; however, seek the advice of your veterinarian as soon as possible. Symptoms of poisoning are often chills, depression and sometimes vomiting; however, vomiting may be caused by the presence of a foreign body or by disease. Vomiting with diarrhea may indicate an advanced state of poisoning. Since diarrhea may be caused by diseases, parasitic, infectious and non-infectious, do not attempt home diagnosis.

Beside the diseases and maladies already mentioned, accidents are always possible, minor ones, such as small abrasions and lacerations and major ones such as automobile accidents. For wounds, household peroxide (three percent) is an effective and safe antiseptic. In any case, if there is any doubt as to the severity of the condition, consult your veterinarian.

Finally, let me say that this tough breed has less trouble with the maladies mentioned than most breeds. The information is meant to enlighten, not to frighten, and so to help you help your dog.

Shall There Be Puppies

You may have bought your Brittany without intending to breed her, but at least one litter is fun for the family and is also good for the female.

Care of your brood bitch begins, not only before she whelps, but before she is bred. Make sure she is in good general health before you breed her. The bitch will come in season for the first time at around eight months. If she is well-grown, matured, above the breed's average age for the first season and in good physical condition, it is generally conceded not to be harmful to breed on the first heat. However, waiting until the second period is generally wiser.

Good breeding condition means that the bitch is neither underweight nor overfat, is free from worms and any major ailment which could be passed on to her nursing puppies. If she is overweight, the chance of getting in whelp is decreased, and whelping difficulties are intensified. Thus, she should be put on a diet before being bred and prevented from gaining too much weight during pregnancy.

If the dam is undernourished, the puppies are not going to be healthy at birth, and, if they survive, will get off to a bad start, which is bound to show up later in bone, substance and finish. If the bitch is infested with worms, worm her before breeding or early in pregnancy. In case she has worms the puppies are likely

Brittanys are hardy and even small puppies can live in outdoor kennels during winter months, providing the building is solid, draft-proof and raised from the damp ground. These puppy houses with front opening leading to the wire-floored runs are easy to clean and practical.

to pick them up at an early age from their surroundings, regardless of whether or not the dam has been wormed, so it is well to check them.

Should the bitch be troubled with a skin or other ailment, make every effort to clear it up before she whelps, as it may infect her puppies, and will be aggravated while nursing, causing her a great deal of suffering.

Choose the stud dog to whom you are going to breed your bitch and make arrangements well in advance. He should counteract as far as possible her faults, and you will be better satisfied in the end if you choose the best dog available instead of economizing. You are expected to take or send the bitch to the stud dog, and it is well to do it in advance of the date when you expect her to be ready, so that his owner can supervise and choose the time for breeding.

When it comes to the actual breeding, time is important. Since the length of season may vary widely between bitches, a specific day cannot be chosen arbitrarily as the right one. If you have ample time and the stud dog is not in great demand, you can breed the bitch between the first day she accepts the dog and the time when she is no longer receptive. However, some bitches may never show signs of willingness and must be force-bred, while others will refuse several dogs but accept another. The vaginal smear method of determining correct breeding time, carried out by your veterinarian, will save wasted matings, misses and disappointments.

During pregnancy it is not advisable to increase the amount of food rapidly as the bitch will put on weight before the extra nourishment is needed by the puppies. However, many breeders believe in the addition of supplements containing calcium and other minerals, and vitamins during pregnancy. While the total amount of food should not be increased, the percentage of meat, eggs, fat, milk, and other protein-rich food is augmented. When the bitch begins to show evidence of being in whelp the amount can be raised, as she will generally develop a ravenous appetite while the puppies are growing. As she becomes weighed down and uncomfortable with a large litter during the last weeks her appetite will lessen. Increase the concentrates and lessen the meal or cereal base of her food, so that she will continue well-nourished while eating less. Tempt her appetite with meat and liver, and milk if she likes it.

Exercise during pregnancy is a much-debated question. The bitch should not be "packed in cotton wool" until she has puppies, but neither should she be forced to exercise more than she is inclined to. Jumping and rough play are definitely out, but many bitches will voluntarily join such activities. During the latter part of pregnancy this should be prevented forcibly if necessary as she can injure herself or her puppies.

The place where the bitch is to whelp should be prepared a week or so in advance, so that she may spend her nights there and become accustomed to the place. Then she will not be uneasy when the time comes; generally she will accept the whelping room or pen and go there when she is going to whelp.

Layers of spread-out newspapers make excellent bedding for the area, in sufficient thickness to provide absorbency, and can be covered over, then picked up and replaced while the old ones are burned.

If the bitch is in whelp, she will start losing the hair around the breasts at least a week before the puppies are due. The area should be kept clean, and washed thoroughly before she whelps.

Be prepared several days in advance for the actual whelping, for the normal period may be sixty to sixty-five days and sixty-one days is as common as sixty-three. The bitch will show uneasiness and discomfort before the puppies arrive. However, the sure way to predict the event is by temperature. Invariably the bitch's temperature will drop from a normal of 101-102 degrees to 99-100 degrees. She will whelp within twelve hours of the fall in temperature. Some bitches will eat regularly until the first puppy makes his appearance, but generally lack of desire to eat even the most tempting food is another indication of approaching birth.

It is a good idea to have a warm place to put the puppies as they are born, for if they are left with the bitch they will generally get wet and cold as each addition to the family arrives. A basket big enough to hold the litter, with sides high enough to prevent drafts may be placed where the bitch can see it to prevent her from worrying. If you have an electric heating pad, it will provide even heat, but keep it turned low and place a flannel or rag over it so that the heat is not too strong for the puppies. Otherwise, a hot water bottle wrapped in a cloth will serve the purpose.

When the first puppy makes its appearance be ready to help if the bitch doesn't seem to know what to do or does not act quickly enough in breaking the sac and licking the puppy to dry and stimulate it. Rubbing with a towel replaces the action of the bitch's tongue, and you can cut the umbilical cord with scissors if she does not bite it herself. Tearing is recommended instead, to prevent bleeding, but the puppy and especially the placenta are slippery to handle at this point. If you wait several minutes and then cut jaggedly, sawing rather than snipping it, no harm is done. Be sure to leave at least two inches of the cord attached to the puppy; it will shrink up when it dries to much less than you would expect. If the bitch seems to be biting too close to the puppy, it is a good idea to take this job away from her as she, too, can do harm, possibly causing hernias or allowing infection to enter. Keep a bottle of alcohol handy to rinse the scissors before use, and iodine in a shallow dish to dip the end of the umbilical cord, as this is more thorough than painting it.

The bitch should be allowed to eat the first one or two of the placentae, or afterbirths, as it stimulates contractions of the uterus and whelping of the remaining puppies. But if she is allowed to dispose of too many in her instinctive efforts to clean the nest, she may become sick and lose her appetite, which does her no good. So remove them and spread fresh newspapers over the messy spot, and she will relax on that score.

Retaining the afterbirth can lead to serious troubles, so keep count and make sure each is passed after the puppy or with the next. If some time has elapsed since the birth of the last puppy and she has not finished "cleaning," call your veterinarian who will take care of the situation. You may think that the bitch is through whelping and all is normal, but if within a day she begins to droop, take her temperature and if it is above normal, indicating the presence of infection, contact the veterinarian immediately.

If the bitch does not proceed with one puppy after another in normal fashion (the puppies should arrive from ten to thirty minutes apart, but intervals of an hour or two are not uncommon), take her outside and the exercise plus a drink of water may encourage matters. If she seems to be in prolonged labor without results, the puppy may be presented backwards or upside down, a so-called "breach." Careful assistance may be given by means of a well-soaped finger to ease the puppy back so that it may turn around to be born normally. If the bitch evidently has more puppies in the offing but shows no sign of producing, and you have tried the walk outside and waited beyond the normal expectation, other action is necessary. It is best to call your veterinarian to make sure all is well and take measures so that another puppy will soon be on its way.

To return to the puppies, try to make sure they get a meal as soon as they are dry, for then they will settle down to sleep peacefully in the warm basket. Keeping them together, warm and dry, in the basket will prevent chills.

Many breeders also keep a baby or grocery scale handy when the puppies are born and weigh them, noting down markings and any outstanding characteristics. The record may be kept up to date with weekly weighing and noting qualities; when you are ready for final selection you will have a better basis for choosing the best pup.

When the bitch is through whelping, take her outside so that she may relieve herself, and meanwhile remove the soiled newspapers and put down a thick fresh layer. It is a good idea to give the puppies better footing than the slippery newspapers. Have a spare to use while you wash one, and the puppies and their mother will be very comfortable, cushioned from the floor.

Keep an eye on the puppies during the first week or two to make sure all are getting their fair share of food. If it is a large litter, you *can* raise them all by keeping half in your heated basket and half with the mother, alternating shifts every two to three hours. It's work, but a much more sensible plan than arbitrarily picking puppies to be destroyed.

It is surprising how fast the puppies learn to be clean. As soon as they can squirm actively and walk a little they will leave their sleeping place to relieve themselves, and then waddle back. Putting a low (two-inch) partition in the pen will generally be enough to make them use one part for sleeping and the other for their "exercise ring."

Feeding the bitch while she is nursing the puppies as a full-time job is generally no problem for she will eat anything and everything. After the puppies are born she should be tempted to drink some warm milk or broth, but she will be ready soon for full-time nourishment and this is one time that you can feed her about as much as she will eat. Two large meals, morning and night, with milk at noon and a snack after her evening run will keep her happy. Be sure to keep fresh water available at all times as she needs a good deal of liquid now and for the weeks to come.

Most people trim their dog's nails but don't think of the puppies'. For the sake of their dam, use nail-clippers on the needle-sharp tips of the puppies' claws when they are two weeks old, and weekly thereafter, to prevent scratching and accidents with long nails. If any long tails appear in the litter your veterinarian will crop them with a simple, almost painless operation to the desirable length, at the same time removing unnecessary dewclaws.

Many people start the weaning process by teaching the puppies to lap warm milk, but they take to solid food much more readily. Runts given a little extra care to bring them along will gobble liver soup or baby food before their eyes are open. Heat a little milk to remove the chill and then mix a saucerful with baby cereal to gruel consistency and feed immediately as it quickly becomes pastelike. The pups will nibble at it when their noses are stuck in. While they spread quite a bit on themselves, their mother's tongue or a damp rag will take care of it, and they are getting the solid food they need at this age. Build up to four meals a day, varying with meat broth and liver soup for the liquid base, and introducing milk to lap when they are better adapted to eating. A meal of ground beef is much enjoyed; even at this age they will growl at each other over tidbits! Dog meal can gradually be mixed with the cereal, or you can start them entirely on one of the puppy foods, but puppies will often turn up their noses at the coarse meal if switched from the baby food too early.

As they eat more food prepared by you the puppies are less dependent on their mother, and she can stay away for longer periods, nursing them only night and morning and finally once a day to relieve pressure as she dries up her milk supply. At this stage cut down on her food to make it easier to decrease the milk supply, but do not starve her. Once she has ceased to manufacture milk, feed her well so she will recover quickly from the strain of lactation.

The puppies will be three weeks old before any worms which they may have picked up develop, but if they are badly infested their growth will be retarded, so have their stools checked and administer the worm medicine your veterinarian recommends, if necessary.

They may now receive immunization for distemper and hepatitis as early as six weeks, and should have these injections, before

they go out into the world I advise this with due consideration.
Your puppies are now on their own, and their mother is ready
for a well-deserved rest for another year.

The Spaying Question

Spaying is a surgical procedure that removes the ovaries from a female dog so that she will never "come into season," cannot be bred and will never have puppies.

Needless to say if you have acquired a female Brittany you have probably done so with the firm intention of breeding her sometime in the future. In that case the question of spaying will never enter your mind. On the other hand for some reason you may want a spayed (not "spaded") female. Remember that if she is spayed and you change your mind about puppies there's nothing you can do about it. Furthermore you may decide to enter your bitch in a dog show. You can enter a spayed bitch in obedience competition but not in conformation classes or in a field trial. You have time to consider the question. Although it has been customary to spay females before they have their first season, it is now being advocated widely in the veterinary profession that it is best to have it done about four months after the female's first season. The reason for this is that the development of the ovaries plays a part in the physical and mental development of the animal. When spayed very young, there is a glandular disharmony. The puppy is more apt to become sluggish and later incline to obesity. If it is done when the pup is more mature and has developed mature interests it has no effect upon her natural characteristics and she never loses them. Spaying is often done quite late in a bitch's life to correct and prevent mammary tumors.

Some people have a horror of the care involved in protecting a bitch in season. It is not at all difficult. Her season will only occur twice a year for a period of about three weeks, six months apart, and once you get the hang of it there's very little trouble. She cannot, and will not, be mated at any other time.

Your female will begin to show a swelling in the vulva at about seven or eight months of age. She may act a little differently, becoming restless or overly affectionate. There will be a discharge that gradually changes to bleeding. This may be very slight or, in some individuals, profuse. About the tenth day the discharge changes to a lighter color and the vulva is conspicuously enlarged. She is most receptive during this stage and extreme care must be taken to avoid an accidental mating. When the vulva shrinks to normal size and the discharge disappears she is out of season. Give her a bath and let her resume her regular social life.

It is the odor of the discharge that attracts male dogs. As soon as your bitch shows signs of coming into season, keep her in the house, preferably locked upstairs or in the basement as dogs have a way of slipping out of opened doors. When you take her out for her daily duties, carry her from your door to your car and drive to some area away from your home before you let her put a foot on the ground. A bitch in season leaves her telltale odor as soon as she urinates which she will have an urge to do often at this time. If there is no odor around your yard, male dogs will just think she's away visiting her grandmother. If you put her down in your yard, she will squat. The next door dog is alerted. He carries the odor on his feet where other dogs detect it and soon you will have a rousing multitude on your doorstep day and night.

If car travel is impossible, walk her to a corner lot a block or two away for her duties but let her wear the neat sanitary pants that are available for bitches in season, or make your own contraption. With or without pants, apply one of the commercial liquids supposed to keep male dogs away, or use plain citronella or smear mentholated salve around her rear end. These products are very useful to disguise the oestrual odor but they will not prevent a male dog from breeding your bitch. There are some dogs which would breed a bitch even if she were standing in a tubful of repellent lotion. Besides, when your bitch wants to accept a male she will let him know quite plainly that she is ready and he will forget citronella. If this still seems like too much trouble, you can usually find a good boarding kennel where she can be lodged.

If your bitch is kenneled outdoors within a wire enclosure, make sure it is "Romeo" proof and escape-proof and keep her there during her entire period. If you take her out for field exercise carry her to and from the kennel and your car.

One thing more. It is your fault if you allow your bitch to advertise her condition. Don't blame the neighbors if their dogs sit on your doorstep, and it is cruel to beat off the dogs. They can't help their natural instincts.

Your Aging Brittany

There is something very heart-warming in the sight of an aged dog that is loved and well-cared for. True, it is sad to realize that you may not have him with you so very much longer, but there is great satisfaction in knowing that you have contributed to his long and happy life by your affection and attention.

At first you won't realize that your dog is getting old. Then, one day you will notice that he has slowed down in his responses; he doesn't seem to hear very well, or is a little slow to recognize you. In the field he becomes less positive on game and you suspect that his "nose" is not as good as usual. He finds it difficult to go up or down the stairs and he gets up stiffly from his nap instead of with his usual bounce. You begin to count the years and you are surprised at the number. They have flown by so swiftly! But now you can do many things for your aging dog to give him a comfortable and healthy old age and, to you, a rewarding one.

First of all, watch your dog's diet. Some Brittanys, like other individuals of spaniel breeds, have a tendency to overeat. Remember that because of reduced activity and metabolic rate, the caloric requirements of the older dog are less. The diet should be complete, but lessen the amounts to avoid obesity. Fat levels should be comparatively low and protein high. Giving supplementary vitamins of the B group and vitamin A will be very helpful to your aged dog.

An elderly dog has less resistance to stress of any kind. He feels temperature changes much more than the youngster. Be sure he has plenty of bedding and a warm place to sleep in chilly weather and shield him from drafts. Perhaps he has been trained to stay off the furniture but in his old age he will love the comfort of a special soft chair to rest in. It isn't too much to ask that he be given some special privileges now and he will thrive on them. Old dogs sometimes forget their training. Don't be harsh, he cannot help it.

Sometimes an older dog will not drink enough water. Try to find some liquid he likes, such as broths or milk to make up for the lack. Constipation may occur. Relieve it when necessary by a dose of milk of magnesia or mineral oil.

If your aged pal's eyesight is dimming, don't let him know it. Keep him where he knows his way around without bumping into misplaced furniture or objects. If he must go up or down stairs give him a helping hand. And, by all means, if you bring a young pup into your home, don't let him torment the old fellow by continual frolicking. Always show your old friend, by your attention and kindness, that he has not been replaced in your affection.

Have your veterinarian give him a check-up about every six months. There may be teeth or gums that need attention, anal gland accumulation or a kidney disorder that can be corrected by treatment. A great many things that were impossible years ago can be done today to lengthen your dog's life. When there is an ear infection that does not respond to treatment there is an operation that can be performed. Tumors can be removed. Elderly female dogs are subject to mammary tumors which can be corrected by surgery or spaying. Aged dogs should not be hospitalized longer than necessary. They are attached to their home and often do much better in familiar surroundings. Your veterinarian will advise you on treating your Brittany at home. The elderly dog needs exercise but it should be moderate so as not to strain his heart. But do take your old hunting companion out occasionally for a short jaunt and shoot a bird for him. He will be so pleased that he is still considered useful!

And if the time comes when there is no other way than to release him from pain and suffering, stay with him to the very end. Don't "send him to the vet's" because you can't bear the final parting. Take him yourself. Your face should be the last sight, the feel of your loving hands, the last thing he knows. Your veterinarian will permit you to be with your pet when he is put quietly and gently into that last, long, deep sleep.

Tribute To A Pal

He was so independent and rugged and strong looking. He wasn't pretty but he had character. Turned out in a big field, instead of running with other young Brittanys, he went his own way, finding it more interesting to search out the alder patches in the far corners. He was roan and heavy-coated; and in comparison with the other pups, he look like a shaggy little bear.

I hadn't intended getting a Brittany pup. My luncheon host was a great Brittany fancier and when I mentioned that "sometime" I might like a Brittany, one about a year old and ready for training, he said, "Let's go take a look at some." And so I went home with Uly; his registered name was Ulysses.

It was a hot August day. The pup had never been in a car before. Not knowing that any dogs would be leaving, the kennel man had fed them all. I had no crate in the car so Uly was on the seat beside me. He had a lot more than butterflies in his stomach, but I thought I could get him home before he began upchucking. I didn't, and since he had been drooling down the back of my neck all the way, his dinner landed over my shoulder and into my lap. Hot, soaked with drool and dirty, with a ruined dress to boot, at that moment I could have parted with him for a nickel. A year later no money could have bought him.

He was a quiet pup and seemed completely at home in his new kennel. Turned out with the other dogs he was friendly enough

There was no "maybe" in Uly's pointing stance. Leaning into the scent told you he had a bird "right there."

but made no special overtures. This type of dog he was.
He was pleasant in a sort of "take me or leave me" way with us, as if he had a great many important things to think about if

he were left alone. We awaited his adulthood with expectation.

Of course, I could hardly wait to see what he would do on game birds; so very soon with two friends and their English setter pups we went to a place where we knew there were pheasants. Uly put on a great show of hunting but when he flushed a bird he never glanced at it, simply went on his way. That was unusual. A bird dog puppy usually chases his very first bird. We went out several times. He continued to be utterly indifferent. Didn't this dog have any nose or interest? I took a lot of kidding from my friends: "Are you sure his name isn't Useless . . . maybe you have to speak French to him." But I wouldn't give up, and let this be a lesson to anyone with a hunting breed pup, sometimes the slow starters make the best dogs.

One day Uly went barging into a big cock bird. It got up with a clatter. Uly went on a few paces, then stopped in his tracks, looked back at the bird and chased it as hard as he could.

That was it. He was a bird dog ever afterwards. Of course, he still had a lot to learn about field manners. He pointed with unusual intensity and became an excellent gun dog.

He was very devoted to all the members of the family. He had no tail to wag but his whole rear would wiggle in greeting. And he had the "smiling" habit of lifting his lip. We would say "Are you happy? Smile, Uly!" and up would go the lip while he almost shook off his hind end. But he never lost his dignity. During his old age when he had a bronchial cough I tried to make him sleep, covered, on my bed on cold nights. He would stay just long enough to be polite and then go to a place on the floor. He never liked soft beds, rugs or even bedding in his kennel. He was a bare floor guy, first and last.

He had a clownish show-off streak, too. He appeared at various times in indoor gun dog demonstrations, (pointing caged birds hidden under brush) at the University Club, the Plaza Hotel (a men's fashion show!) and Rockefeller Center. It got so that whenever he entered a building in New York City he would start pointing, birds or not, just to show off. One time I drove in from the country with some live pheasants in a covered cage on the floor of the car and Uly on the back seat. When I was stopped by red lights I noticed people staring into the rear of the car so I looked back. There was Uly standing on the seat, frozen into a point. I often wished that he would be as steady in the field!

*Even a boy long remembers a pleasant association. Who can tell,
perhaps they remember the longest!*

On a shoot one time I walked over to greet an arrival just letting his three pointers out of his car. They dashed, en masse, up to Uly who gave them one long look and growled menacingly. They backed off and Uly pursued his way. Our friend was amazed. "I never knew a Brittany would be that brave," he said. "You don't know Brittanys," I answered. But I didn't add that Uly had been raised with pointers. Big dogs were old stuff to him. He was especially devoted to one pointer and they were great pals. Don't let anyone tell you that two dogs or two bitches kenneled together will always fight. Sometimes, yes. But I have seen such solid friendships between two females and between dogs that they could hardly bear to be parted.

The
Ideal
Brittany

General description—A compact, closely knit dog of medium size, a leggy spaniel having the appearance as well as the agility of a great ground coverer. Strong, vigorous, energetic and quick of movement. Not too light in bone, yet never heavy boned and cumbersome. Ruggedness, without clumsiness, is a characteristic of the breed. So leggy is he that his height at the withers is the same as the length of his body. He has no tail, or at most, not more than four inches.

Weight—Should weigh between thirty and forty pounds.

Height—Seventeen and one-half to twenty and one-half inches—measured from the ground to the highest point of the back—the withers.

Disqualifications—Any Brittany spaniel measuring under seventeen and one-half inches or over twenty and one-half inches shall be disqualified from bench show competition. Any black in the coat or a nose so dark in color as to appear black shall disqualify. A tail substantially more than four inches in length shall disqualify.

Coat—Hair dense, flat or wavy, never curly. Not as fine as in other spaniel breeds, and never silky. Furnishings not profuse. The ears should carry little fringe. Neither the front nor hind legs should carry heavy featherings.

Note: Long, curly, or silky hair is a fault. Any tendency toward excessive feathering should be severely penalized, as undesirable in a sporting dog which must face burrs and heavy cover.

Skin—Fine and fairly loose. (A loose skin rolls with briars and sticks, thus diminishing punctures or tearing. But a skin so loose as to form pouches is undesirable.)

Color—Dark orange and white, or liver and white. Some ticking is desirable, but not so much as to produce belton patterns. Roan patterns or factors of orange or liver shade are permissible. The orange and liver are found in standard particolor, or piebald patterns. Washed out or faded colors are not desirable. Black is a disqualification.

Skull—Medium length (approximately four and three-fourths inches). Rounded, very slightly wedge shaped, but evenly made. Width, not quite as wide as the length (about four and three-eights inches) and never so broad as to appear coarse, or so narrow as to appear racy. Well-defined, but gently sloping stop effect. Median line rather indistinct. The occipital crest only apparent to the touch. Lateral walls well rounded. The Brittany should never be "apple-headed" and he should never have an indented stop. (All measurements of skull are for a nineteen and one-half inch dog.)

Muzzle—Medium length, about two-thirds the length of the skull, measuring the muzzle from the tip to the stop, and the skull from the occipital crest to the stop between the eyes. Muzzle should taper gradually in both horizontal and vertical dimensions as it approaches the nostrils. Neither a Roman nose nor a concave curve (dish-face) is desirable. Never broad, heavy, or snipey.

Nose—Nostrils well open to permit deep breathing of air and adequate scenting while at top speed. Tight nostrils should be penalized. Never shiny. Color, fawn, tan, light shades of brown or deep pink. A black nose is a disqualification. A two-tone or butterfly nose should be severely penalized.

Eyes—Well set in head. Well protected from briars by a heavy, expressive eyebrow. A prominent, full or pop eye should be heavily penalized. It is a serious fault in a hunting dog that must face briars. Skull well chiseled under the eyes, so that the lower lid is not pulled back to form a pocket or haw for catching seeds, dirt and weed dust. Judges should check by forcing head down to see if lid falls away from the eye. Preference should be for darker colored eyes, though lighter shades of amber should not be penalized. Light and mean-looking eyes to be penalized.

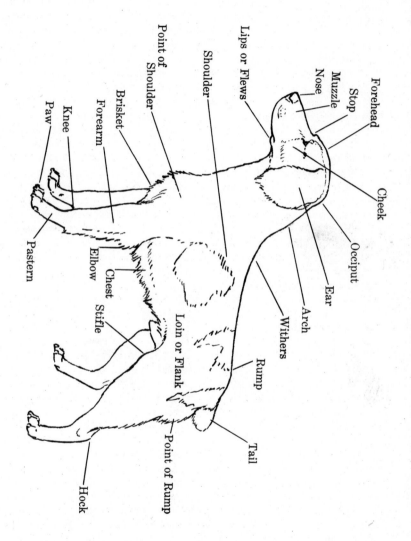

Forehead
Stop
Muzzle
Nose
Lips or Flews
Shoulder
Point of Shoulder
Brisket
Forearm
Knee
Paw
Pastern
Elbow
Chest
Stifle
Hock
Point of Rump
Loin or Flank
Rump
Tail
Withers
Arch
Ear
Occiput
Cheek

Ears—Set high, above the level of the eyes. Short and leafy, rather than pendulous, reaching about half the lenth of the muzzle. Should lie flat and close to the head, with the tip rounded very slightly. Ears well covered with dense, but relatively short hair, and with little fringe.

Lips—Tight to the muzzle, with the upper lip overlapping the lower jaw only sufficiently to cover under lip. Lips dry so that feathers do not stick. Drooling to receive a heavy penalty. Flews to be penalized.

Teeth—Well joined incisors. Posterior edge of upper incisors in contact with anterior edge of lower incisors, thus giving a true scissors bite. Overshot or undershot jaw to be penalized heavily.

Neck—Medium length. Not quite permitting the dog to place his nose on the ground without bending his legs. Free from throatiness, though not a serious fault unless accompanied by dewlaps. Strong, without giving the impression of being over-muscled. Well set into sloping shoulders. Never concave or ewe-necked.

Body length—Approximately the same as the height when measured at the withers. Body length is measured from the point of the forechest to the rear of the haunches. A long body should be heavily penalized.

Withers—Shoulder blades should not protrude much. Not too widely set apart with perhaps two thumbs' width or less between the blades. At the withers, the Brittany is slightly higher than at the rump.

Shoulders—Sloping and muscular. Blade and upper arm should form nearly a ninety-degree angle when measured from the posterior point of the blade at the withers to the junction of the blade and upper arm, and thence to the point of the elbow nearest the ribs. Straight shoulders do not permit sufficient reach.

Back—Short and straight. Slight slope from highest point of withers to the root of the tail. Distance from last rib to upper thigh short, about three to four finger widths.

Chest—Deep, reaching the level of the elbow. Neither so wide nor so rounded as to disturb the placement of the shoulder bones and elbows, which causes a paddling movement, and often causes soreness from elbow striking ribs. Ribs well sprung, but adequate heart room provided by depth as well as width. Narrow or slab-sided chests are a fault.

Flank—Rounded. Fairly full. Not extremely tucked up, nor yet flabby and falling. Loins short and strong. Narrow and weak loins are a fault. In motion the loin should not sway sideways, giving a zigzag motion to the back, wasting energy.

Hindquarters—Broad, strong and muscular, with powerful thighs and well-bent stifles, giving a hip set well into the loin and the marked angulation necessary for a powerful drive when in motion. Fat and falling hindquarters are a fault.

Tail—Naturally tail-less, or not over four inches long. Natural or docked. Set on high, actually an extension of the spine at about the same level.

Front legs—Viewed from the front, perpendicular, but not set too wide as in the case of a dog loaded in shoulder. Elbows and feet turning neither in nor out. Viewed from the side, practically perpendicular to the pastern. Pastern slightly bent to give cushion to stride. Not so straight as in terriers. Falling pasterns, however, are a serious fault. Leg bones clean, graceful, but not too fine. An extremely heavy bone is as much as fault as spindly legs. One must look for substance and suppleness. Height to the elbows should approximately equal distance from elbow to withers.

Hind legs—Stifles well bent. The stifle generally is the term used for knee joint. If the angle made by the upper and lower leg bones is too straight, the dog quite generally lacks drive, since his hind legs cannot drive as far forward at each stride as is desirable. However, the stifle should not be bent as to throw the hock joint far out behind the dog. Since factors not easily seen by the eye may give the dog his proper drive, a Brittany should not be condemned for straight stifle until the judge has checked the dog in motion from the side. When at a trot, the Brittany's hind foot should step into or beyond the print left by the front foot.

The stifle joint should not turn out making a cowhock. (The cowhock moves the foot out to the side, thus driving out of line, and losing reach at each stride.) Thighs well feathered, but not profusely, halfway to the hock. Hocks, that is, the back pasterns, should be moderately short, pointing neither in nor out; perpendicular when viewed from the side. They should be firm when shaken by the judge.

Feet—Should be strong, proportionately smaller than other spaniels, with close-fitting, well-arched toes and thick pads. The Brittany is not "up on his toes." Toes not heavily feathered. Flat feet, splayed feet, paper feet, etc., are to be heavily penalized. An ideal foot is halfway between the hare- and cat-foot.

Disqualifications—Any Brittany measuring under seventeen and one-half inches or over twenty and one-half inches. Any black in the coat or a nose so dark as to appear black. A tail substantially more than four inches in length.

Approved November 18, 1952

Breed Magazine

The American Brittany, published by the American Brittany Club. Issued to all members of the American Brittany Club, numbering about 3,000.

Breed Club

The American Brittany Club, Walter B. Kleeman, secretary, 21 South Fountain, Springfield, Ohio.

American Kennel Club, 221 Fourth Avenue, New York 3, N.Y.